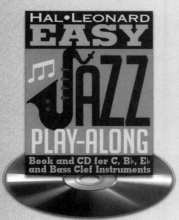

HAL•LEONARD

EASY

JAZZ

PLAY•ALONG

Book and CD for C, Bb, Eb
and Bass Clef Instruments

FIRST JAZZ SONGS

18 Classics
for Beginning Jazz Musicians

Recorded by Ric Probst at Tanner Monagle Studio
Piano: Mark Davis
Bass: Tom McGirr
Drums: Dave Bayles

ISBN 978-1-4584-1510-3

HAL•LEONARD®
CORPORATION
7777 W. BLUEMOUND RD. P.O. BOX 13819 MILWAUKEE, WI 53213

Visit Hal Leonard Online at
www.halleonard.com

CONTENTS

All of Me

C Version

Words and Music by Seymour Simons
and Gerald Marks

All the Things You Are

from *Very Warm for May*

C Version

Lyrics by Oscar Hammerstein II
Music by Jerome Kern

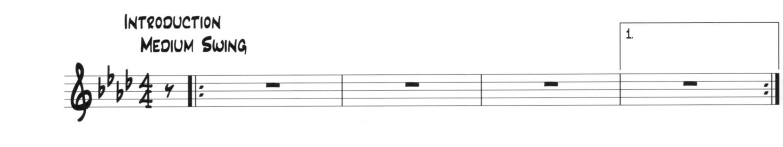

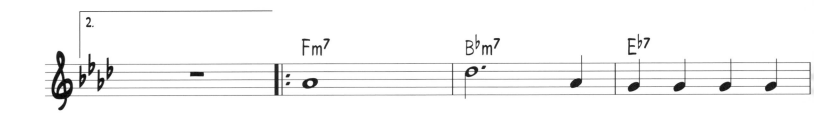

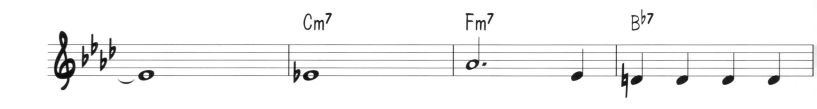

AUTUMN LEAVES

C VERSION

English Lyric by Johnny Mercer
French Lyric by Jacques Prevert
Music by Joseph Kosma

C-Jam Blues

C Version

By Duke Ellington

COMIN' HOME BABY

C Version

Words and Music by Robert Dorough
and Benjamin Tucker

Footprints

C Version

By Wayne Shorter

IN A MELLOW TONE

C Version

By Duke Ellington

THE GIRL FROM IPANEMA
(Garôta de Ipanema)

C Version

Music by Antonio Carlos Jobim
English Words by Norman Gimbel
Original Words by Vinicius de Moraes

KILLER JOE

By Benny Golson

C Version

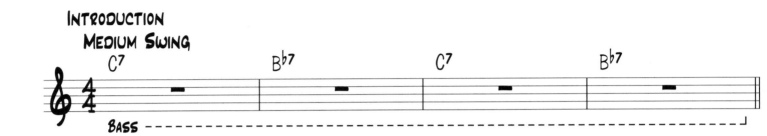

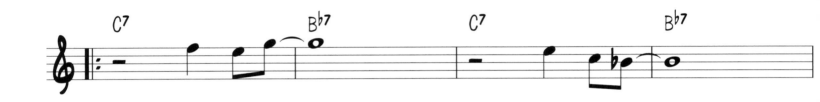

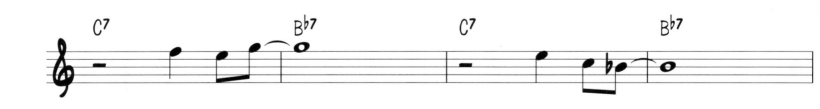

LITTLE SUNFLOWER

C VERSION

By Freddie Hubbard

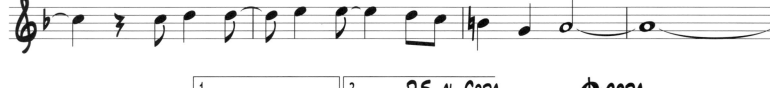

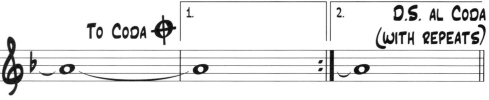

Mr. P.C.

C Version

By John Coltrane

MILESTONES

C VERSION

By Miles Davis

ON GREEN DOLPHIN STREET

C Version

Lyrics by Ned Washington
Music by Bronislau Kaper

One For Daddy-O

C VERSION

By Nat Adderley

Reunion Blues

C Version

By Milt Jackson

TUNE UP

C VERSION

By Miles Davis

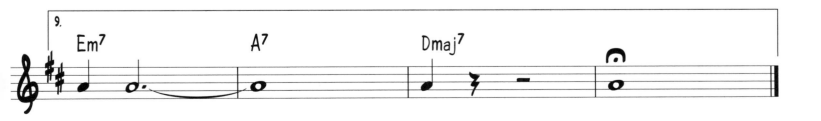

Satin Doll
FROM SOPHISTICATED LADIES

C VERSION

By Duke Ellington

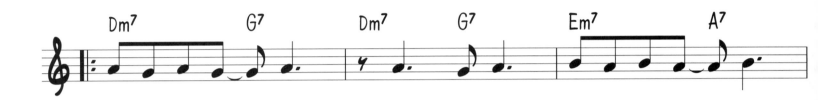

There Will Never Be Another You

FROM THE MOTION PICTURE ICELAND

C VERSION

LYRIC BY MACK GORDON
MUSIC BY HARRY WARREN

All of Me

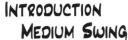

Words and Music by Seymour Simons
and Gerald Marks

All the Things You Are

FROM VERY WARM FOR MAY

Bb VERSION

LYRICS BY OSCAR HAMMERSTEIN II
MUSIC BY JEROME KERN

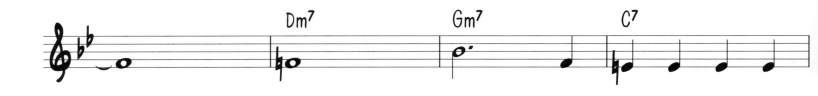

33

AUTUMN LEAVES

B♭ VERSION

ENGLISH LYRIC BY JOHNNY MERCER
FRENCH LYRIC BY JACQUES PREVERT
MUSIC BY JOSEPH KOSMA

C-Jam Blues

B♭ Version

By Duke Ellington

Medium Swing

Copyright © 1942 Sony/ATV Music Publishing LLC in the U.S.A.
Copyright Renewed
This arrangement Copyright © 2012 Sony/ATV Music Publishing LLC in the U.S.A.
All Rights Administered by Sony/ATV Music Publishing LLC, 8 Music Square West, Nashville, TN 37203
Rights for the world outside the U.S.A. Administered by EMI Robbins Catalog Inc. (Publishing) and Alfred Publishing Co., Inc. (Print)
International Copyright Secured   All Rights Reserved

Comin' Home Baby

Bb Version

Words and Music by Robert Dorough and Benjamin Tucker

INTRODUCTION
SOUL JAZZ

Footprints

Bb Version

By Wayne Shorter

IN A MELLOW TONE

Bb Version

By Duke Ellington

THE GIRL FROM IPANEMA
(GARÔTA DE IPANEMA)

Bb VERSION

MUSIC BY ANTONIO CARLOS JOBIM
ENGLISH WORDS BY NORMAN GIMBEL
ORIGINAL WORDS BY VINICIUS DE MORAES

42

Killer Joe

Bb Version

By Benny Golson

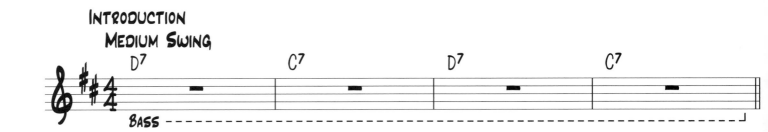

43

LITTLE SUNFLOWER

Bb VERSION

By Freddie Hubbard

Mr. P.C.

Bb Version

By John Coltrane

MILESTONES

Bb VERSION

By Miles Davis

Fast Swing

ON GREEN DOLPHIN STREET

Bb Version

Lyrics by Ned Washington
Music by Bronislau Kaper

ONE FOR DADDY-O

Bb Version

By Nat Adderley

Reunion Blues

Bb Version

By Milt Jackson

Tune Up

B♭ Version

By Miles Davis

Satin Doll
from Sophisticated Ladies

Bb Version

By Duke Ellington

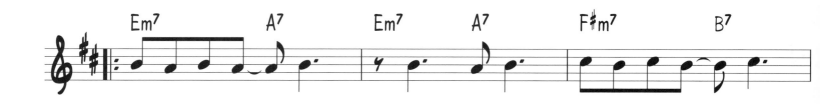

There Will Never Be Another You

FROM THE MOTION PICTURE ICELAND

Bb VERSION

LYRIC BY MACK GORDON
MUSIC BY HARRY WARREN

MEDIUM SWING

All of Me

E♭ Version

Words and Music by Seymour Simons
and Gerald Marks

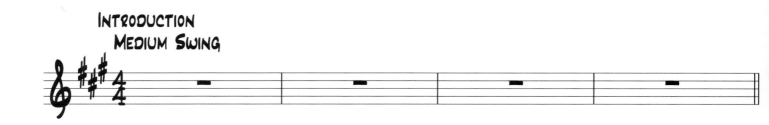

All the Things You Are

from Very Warm for May

Eb Version

Lyrics by Oscar Hammerstein II
Music by Jerome Kern

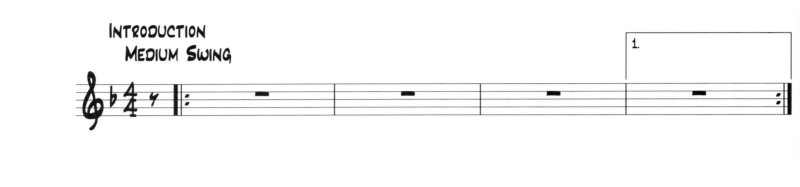

AUTUMN LEAVES

E♭ Version

English lyric by Johnny Mercer
French lyric by Jacques Prévert
Music by Joseph Kosma

C-Jam Blues

Eb Version

By Duke Ellington

Comin' Home Baby

Eb Version

Words and Music by Robert Dorough
and Benjamin Tucker

Footprints

E♭ Version

By Wayne Shorter

In A Mellow Tone

Eb Version

By Duke Ellington

THE GIRL FROM IPANEMA
(Garôta de Ipanema)

Eb Version

Music by Antonio Carlos Jobim
English Words by Norman Gimbel
Original Words by Vinicius de Moraes

Killer Joe

E♭ Version

By Benny Golson

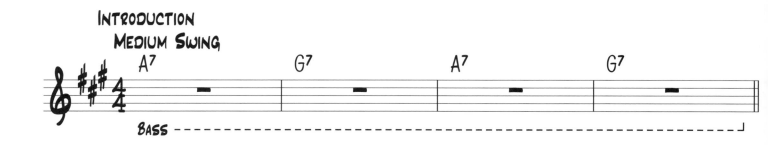

LITTLE SUNFLOWER

Eb VERSION

By Freddie Hubbard

MR. P.C.

By John Coltrane

Eb Version

MILESTONES

Eb Version

By Miles Davis

ON GREEN DOLPHIN STREET

E♭ Version

Lyrics by Ned Washington
Music by Bronislau Kaper

ONE FOR DADDY-O

E♭ VERSION

By Nat Adderley

Reunion Blues

Eᵇ Version

By Milt Jackson

TUNE UP

Eb VERSION

By Miles Davis

Satin Doll
From Sophisticated Ladies

E♭ Version

By Duke Ellington

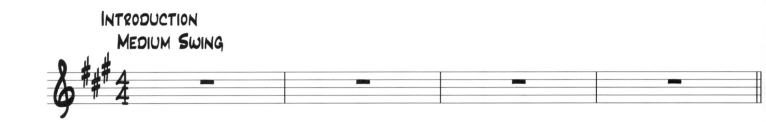

There Will Never Be Another You

FROM THE MOTION PICTURE ICELAND

Eb Version

LYRIC BY MACK GORDON
MUSIC BY HARRY WARREN

Medium Swing

All Of Me

♭ Version

Words and Music by Seymour Simons
and Gerald Marks

Introduction
Medium Swing

All the Things You Are

from VERY WARM FOR MAY

℃ Version

Lyrics by Oscar Hammerstein II
Music by Jerome Kern

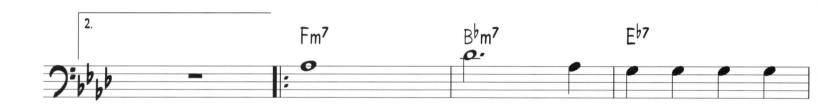

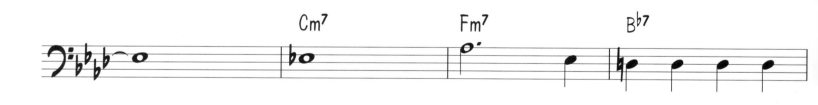

AUTUMN LEAVES

𝄢 VERSION

English Lyric by Johnny Mercer
French Lyric by Jacques Prévert
Music by Joseph Kosma

C-Jam Blues

♭ Version

By Duke Ellington

Comin' Home Baby

FOOTPRINTS

By Wayne Shorter

IN A MELLOW TONE

♭: VERSION

By Duke Ellington

THE GIRL FROM IPANEMA
(Garôta de Ipanema)

🎼 Version

Music by Antonio Carlos Jobim
English Words by Norman Gimbel
Original Words by Vinicius de Moraes

Medium Bossa Nova

D7
Gm7
Eb7
Am7
D7
Gm7
C7
Fmaj7
G7
Gm7
Gb7
1., 2.
Fmaj7
Gb7
3.
Fmaj7
Gb7
Fmaj7
Gb7
Fmaj7
Gb7
Fmaj7

Killer Joe

: Version

By Benny Golson

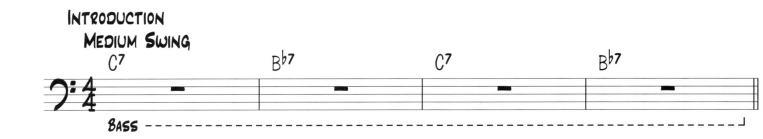

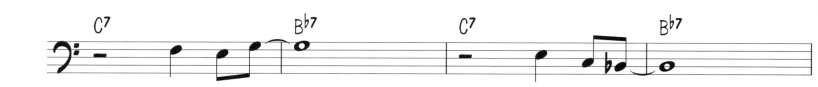

LITTLE SUNFLOWER

Bass Version

By Freddie Hubbard

Mr. P.C.

♭ Version

By John Coltrane

MILESTONES

♭ Version

By Miles Davis

On Green Dolphin Street

Lyrics by Ned Washington
Music by Bronislau Kaper

ONE FOR DADDY-O

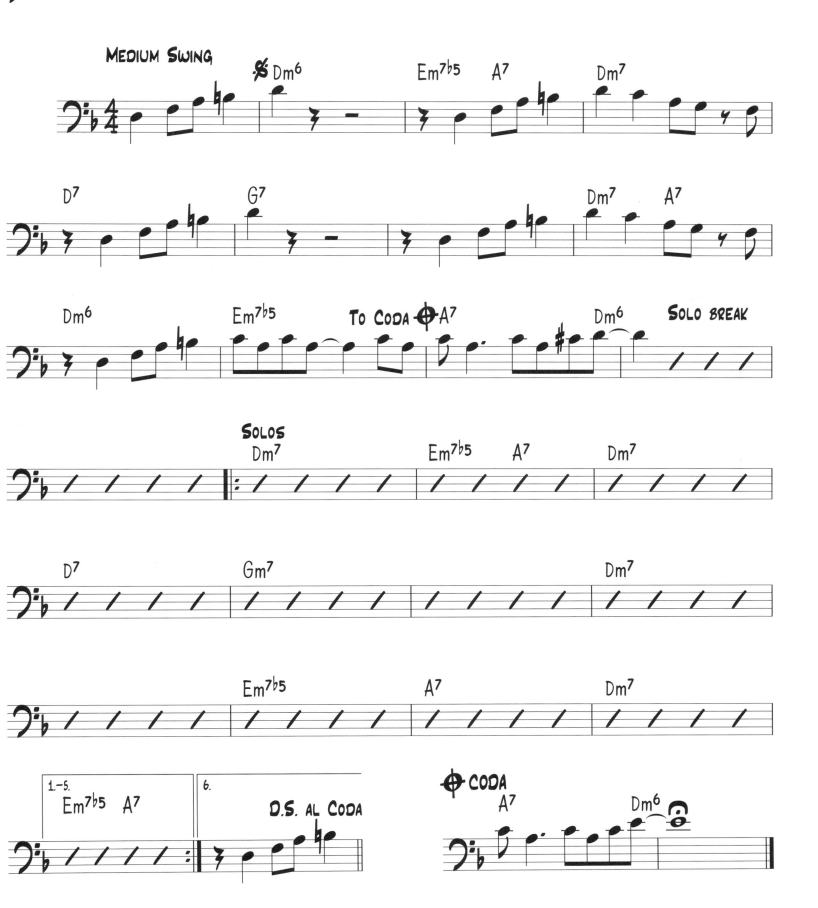

Reunion Blues

C Version

By Milt Jackson

TUNE UP

♭ VERSION

By Miles Davis

Satin Doll
from Sophisticated Ladies

𝄢 Version

By Duke Ellington

Introduction
Medium Swing

There Will Never Be Another You

from the Motion Picture ICELAND

𝄢 Version

Lyric by Mack Gordon
Music by Harry Warren

Presenting the Hal Leonard JAZZ PLAY-ALONG SERIES

For use with all B-flat, E-flat, Bass Clef and C instruments, the Jazz Play-Along® Series is the ultimate learning tool for all jazz musicians. With musician-friendly lead sheets, melody cues, and other split-track choices on the included CD, these first-of-a-kind packages help you master improvisation while playing some of the greatest tunes of all time. FOR STUDY, each tune includes a split track with: melody cue with proper style and inflection • professional rhythm tracks • choruses for soloing • removable bass part • removable piano part. FOR PERFORMANCE, each tune also has: an additional full stereo accompaniment track (no melody) • additional choruses for soloing.

63. CLASSICAL JAZZ
00843064 ....$14.95

64. TV TUNES
00843065 ....$14.95

65. SMOOTH JAZZ
00843066 ....$16.99

66. A CHARLIE BROWN CHRISTMAS
00843067 ....$16.99

67. CHICK COREA
00843068 ....$15.95

68. CHARLES MINGUS
00843069 ....$16.95

69. CLASSIC JAZZ
00843071 ....$15.99

70. THE DOORS
00843072 ....$14.95

71. COLE PORTER CLASSICS
00843073 ....$14.95

72. CLASSIC JAZZ BALLADS
00843074 ....$15.99

73. JAZZ/BLUES
00843075 ....$14.95

74. BEST JAZZ CLASSICS
00843076 ....$15.99

75. PAUL DESMOND
00843077 ....$14.95

76. BROADWAY JAZZ BALLADS
00843078 ....$15.99

77. JAZZ ON BROADWAY
00843079 ....$15.99

78. STEELY DAN
00843070 ....$14.99

79. MILES DAVIS CLASSICS
00843081 ....$15.99

80. JIMI HENDRIX
00843083 ....$15.99

81. FRANK SINATRA – CLASSICS
00843084 ....$15.99

82. FRANK SINATRA – STANDARDS
00843085 ....$15.99

83. ANDREW LLOYD WEBBER
00843104 ....$14.95

84. BOSSA NOVA CLASSICS
00843105 ....$14.95

85. MOTOWN HITS
00843109 ....$14.95

86. BENNY GOODMAN
00843110 ....$14.95

87. DIXIELAND
00843111 ....$14.95

88. DUKE ELLINGTON FAVORITES
00843112 ....$14.95

89. IRVING BERLIN FAVORITES
00843113 ....$14.95

90. THELONIOUS MONK CLASSICS
00841262 ....$16.99

91. THELONIOUS MONK FAVORITES
00841263 ....$16.99

92. LEONARD BERNSTEIN
00450134 ....$15.99

93. DISNEY FAVORITES
00843142 ....$14.99

94. RAY
00843143 ....$14.99

95. JAZZ AT THE LOUNGE
00843144 ....V$14.99

96. LATIN JAZZ STANDARDS
00843145 ....$14.99

97. MAYBE I'M AMAZED*
00843148 ....$15.99

98. DAVE FRISHBERG
00843149 ....$15.99

99. SWINGING STANDARDS
00843150 ....$14.99

100. LOUIS ARMSTRONG
00740423 ....$15.99

101. BUD POWELL
00843152 ....$14.99

102. JAZZ POP
00843153 ....$14.99

**103. ON GREEN DOLPHIN STREET
& OTHER JAZZ CLASSICS**
00843154 ....$14.99

104. ELTON JOHN
00843155 ....$14.99

105. SOULFUL JAZZ
00843151 ....$15.99

106. SLO' JAZZ
00843117 ....$14.99

107. MOTOWN CLASSICS
00843116 ....$14.99

108. JAZZ WALTZ
00843159 ....$15.99

109. OSCAR PETERSON
00843160 ....$16.99

110. JUST STANDARDS
00843161 ....$15.99

111. COOL CHRISTMAS
00843162 ....$15.99

112. PAQUITO D'RIVERA – LATIN JAZZ*
48020662 ....$16.99

113. PAQUITO D'RIVERA – BRAZILIAN JAZZ*
48020663 ....$19.99

114. MODERN JAZZ QUARTET FAVORITES
00843163 ....$15.99

115. THE SOUND OF MUSIC
00843164 ....$15.99

116. JACO PASTORIUS
00843165 ....$15.99

117. ANTONIO CARLOS JOBIM – MORE HITS
00843166 ....$15.99

118. BIG JAZZ STANDARDS COLLECTION
00843167 ....$27.50

119. JELLY ROLL MORTON
00843168 ....$15.99

120. J.S. BACH
00843169 ....$15.99

121. DJANGO REINHARDT
00843170 ....$15.99

122. PAUL SIMON
00843182 ....$16.99

123. BACHARACH & DAVID
00843185 ....$15.99

124. JAZZ-ROCK HORN HITS
00843186 ....$15.99

126. COUNT BASIE CLASSICS
00843157 ....$15.99

127. CHUCK MANGIONE
00843188 ....$15.99

132. STAN GETZ ESSENTIALS
00843193 ....$15.99

133. STAN GETZ FAVORITES
00843194 ....$15.99

134. NURSERY RHYMES*
00843196 ....$17.99

135. JEFF BECK
00843197 ....$15.99

136. NAT ADDERLEY
00843198 ....$15.99

137. WES MONTGOMERY
00843199 ....$15.99

138. FREDDIE HUBBARD
00843200 ....$15.99

139. JULIAN "CANNONBALL" ADDERLEY
00843201 ....$15.99

141. BILL EVANS STANDARDS
00843156 ....$15.99

150. JAZZ IMPROV BASICS
00843195 ....$19.99

151. MODERN JAZZ QUARTET CLASSICS
00843209 ....$15.99

157. HYMNS
00843217 ....$15.99

162. BIG CHRISTMAS COLLECTION
00843221 ....$24.99

*These CDs do not include split tracks.

IMPROVING IS EASIER THAN EVER

with this new series for beginning jazz musicians. The Hal Leonard Easy Jazz Play-Along Series includes songs with accessible chord changes and features recordings with novice-friendly tempos. Just follow the streamlined lead sheets in the book and play along with the professionally recorded backing tracks on the CD. The bass or piano can also be removed by turning down the volume on the left or right channel. The audio CD is playable on any CD player. For PC and Mac computer users, the CD is enhanced so you can adjust the recording to any tempo without changing pitch!

1. FIRST JAZZ SONGS
Book/CD Pack

All of Me • All the Things You Are • Autumn Leaves • C-Jam Blues • Comin' Home Baby • Footprints • The Girl from Ipanema (Garôta De Ipanema) • Killer Joe • Little Sunflower • Milestones • Mr. P.C. • On Green Dolphin Street • One for Daddy-O • Reunion Blues • Satin Doll • There Will Never Be Another You • Tune Up • Watermelon Man.

00843225 B♭, E♭, C & Bass Clef Instruments...............$19.99

3. VITAL JAZZ CLASSICS
Book/CD Pack

Afternoon in Paris • Doxy • 500 Miles High • Girl Talk • Holy Land • Impressions • In Walked Bud • The Jive Samba • Lady Bird • Maiden Voyage • Mercy, Mercy, Mercy • My Little Suede Shoes • Recorda-Me • St. Thomas • Solar • Song for My Father • Stolen Moments • Sunny.

00843227 B♭, E♭, C & Bass Clef Instruments...............$19.99

2. STANDARDS FOR STARTERS
Book/CD Pack

Don't Get Around Much Anymore • Exactly like You • Fly Me to the Moon (In Other Words) • Have You Met Miss Jones? • Honeysuckle Rose • I Remember You • If I Should Lose You • It Could Happen to You • Moon River • My Favorite Things • On a Slow Boat to China • Out of Nowhere • Softly As in a Morning Sunrise • Speak Low • The Very Thought of You • Watch What Happens • The Way You Look Tonight • Yesterdays.

00843226 B♭, E♭, C & Bass Clef Instruments...............$19.99

4. BASIC BLUES
Book/CD Pack

All Blues • Birk's Works • Bloomdido • Blue Seven • Blue Train (Blue Trane) • Blues in the Closet • Cousin Mary • Freddie Freeloader • The Jody Grind • Jumpin' with Symphony Sid • Nostalgia in Times Square • Now See How You Are • Now's the Time • Sonnymoon for Two • Tenor Madness • Things Ain't What They Used to Be • Turnaround • Two Degrees East, Three Degrees West.

00843228 B♭, E♭, C & Bass Clef Instruments...............$19.99

HAL•LEONARD® CORPORATION
7777 W. BLUEMOUND RD. P.O. BOX 13819 MILWAUKEE, WI 53213

Prices, content, and availability subject to change without notice.

HAL•LEONARD BLUES PLAY-ALONG

For use with all the C, B♭, Bass Clef and E♭ Instruments, the Hal Leonard Blues Play-Along Series is the ultimate jamming tool for all blues musicians.

With easy-to-read lead sheets, and other split-track choices on the included CD, these first-of-a-kind packages will bring your local blues jam right into your house! Each song on the CD includes two tracks: a full stereo mix, and a split track mix with removable guitar, bass, piano, and harp parts. The CD is playable on any CD player, and is also enhanced so Mac and PC users can adjust the recording to any tempo without changing the pitch!

1. Chicago Blues
All Your Love (I Miss Loving) • Easy Baby • I Ain't Got You • I'm Your Hoochie Coochie Man • Killing Floor • Mary Had a Little Lamb • Messin' with the Kid • Sweet Home Chicago.
00843106 Book/CD Pack $12.99

2. Texas Blues
Hide Away • If You Love Me Like You Say • Mojo Hand • Okie Dokie Stomp • Pride and Joy • Reconsider Baby • T-Bone Shuffle • The Things That I Used to Do.
00843107 Book/CD Pack $12.99

3. Slow Blues
Don't Throw Your Love on Me So Strong • Five Long Years • I Can't Quit You Baby • I Just Want to Make Love to You • The Sky Is Crying • (They Call It) Stormy Monday (Stormy Monday Blues) • Sweet Little Angel • Texas Flood.
00843108 Book/CD Pack $12.99

4. Shuffle Blues
Beautician Blues • Bright Lights, Big City • Further on up the Road • I'm Tore Down • Juke • Let Me Love You Baby • Look at Little Sister • Rock Me Baby.
00843171 Book/CD Pack $12.99

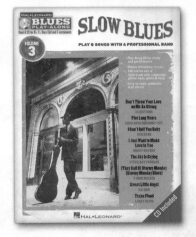

5. B.B. King
Everyday I Have the Blues • It's My Own Fault Darlin' • Just Like a Woman • Please Accept My Love • Sweet Sixteen • The Thrill Is Gone • Why I Sing the Blues • You Upset Me Baby.
00843172 Book/CD Pack $14.99

6. Jazz Blues
Birk's Works • Blues in the Closet • Cousin Mary • Freddie Freeloader • Now's the Time • Tenor Madness • Things Ain't What They Used to Be • Turnaround.
00843175 Book/CD Pack $12.99

7. Howlin' Wolf
Built for Comfort • Forty-Four • How Many More Years • Killing Floor • Moanin' at Midnight • Shake for Me • Sitting on Top of the World • Smokestack Lightning.
00843176 Book/CD Pack $12.99

8. Blues Classics
Baby, Please Don't Go • Boom Boom • Born Under a Bad Sign • Dust My Broom • How Long, How Long Blues • I Ain't Superstitious • It Hurts Me Too • My Babe.
00843177 Book/CD Pack $12.99

9. Albert Collins
Brick • Collins' Mix • Don't Lose Your Cool • Frost Bite • Frosty • I Ain't Drunk • Master Charge • Trash Talkin'.
00843178 Book/CD Pack $12.99

10. Uptempo Blues
Cross Road Blues (Crossroads) • Give Me Back My Wig • Got My Mo Jo Working • The House Is Rockin' • Paying the Cost to Be the Boss • Rollin' and Tumblin' • Turn on Your Love Light • You Can't Judge a Book by the Cover.
00843179 Book/CD Pack $12.99

11. Christmas Blues
Back Door Santa • Blue Christmas • Dig That Crazy Santa Claus • Merry Christmas, Baby • Please Come Home for Christmas • Santa Baby • Soulful Christmas.
00843203 Book/CD Pack $12.99

12. Jimmy Reed
Ain't That Lovin' You Baby • Baby, What You Want Me to Do • Big Boss Man • Bright Lights, Big City • Going to New York • Honest I Do • You Don't Have to Go • You Got Me Dizzy.
00843204 Book/CD Pack $12.99

FOR MORE INFORMATION, SEE YOUR LOCAL MUSIC DEALER, OR WRITE TO:

HAL•LEONARD® CORPORATION
7777 W. BLUEMOUND RD. P.O. BOX 13819 MILWAUKEE, WI 53213

Prices, content, and availability subject to change without notice.

www.halleonard.com

The Best-Selling Jazz Book of All Time Is Now Legal!

The Real Books are the most popular jazz books of all time. Since the 1970s, musicians have trusted these volumes to get them through every gig, night after night. The problem is that the books were illegally produced and distributed, without any regard to copyright law, or royalties paid to the composers who created these musical masterpieces.

Hal Leonard is very proud to present the first legitimate and legal editions of these books ever produced. You won't even notice the difference, other than all the notorious errors being fixed: the covers and typeface look the same, the song lists are nearly identical, and the price for our edition is even cheaper than the originals!

Every conscientious musician will appreciate that these books are now produced accurately and ethically, benefitting the songwriters that we owe for some of the greatest tunes of all time!

VOLUME 1
00240221	C Edition	$32.50
00240224	B♭ Edition	$32.50
00240225	E♭ Edition	$32.50
00240226	Bass Clef Edition	$32.50
00240292	C Edition 6 x 9	$27.95
00451087	C Edition on CD-ROM	$25.00
00240302	A-D Play-Along CDs	$24.99
00240303	E-J Play-Along CDs	$24.95
00240304	L-R Play-Along CDs	$24.95
00240305	S-Z Play-Along CDs	$24.99

VOLUME 2
00240222	C Edition	$29.99
00240227	B♭ Edition	$32.50
00240228	E♭ Edition	$32.50
00240229	Bass Clef Edition	$32.50
00240293	C Edition 6 x 9	$27.95
00240351	A-D Play-Along CDs	$24.99
00240352	E-I Play-Along CDs	$24.99
00240353	J-R Play-Along CDs	$24.99
00240354	S-Z Play-Along CDs	$24.99

VOLUME 3
00240233	C Edition	$32.50
00240284	B♭ Edition	$29.95
00240285	E♭ Edition	$29.95
00240286	Bass Clef Edition	$29.95

VOLUME 4
00240296	C Edition	$29.99

VOLUME 5
00240349	C Edition	$32.50

Also available:
00240264	The Real Blues Book	$34.99
00310910	The Real Bluegrass Book	$29.99
00240137	Miles Davis Real Book	$19.95
00240355	The Real Dixieland Book	$29.99
00240235	The Duke Ellington Real Book	$19.99
00240358	The Charlie Parker Real Book	$19.99
00240331	The Bud Powell Real Book	$19.99
00240313	The Real Rock Book	$29.99
00240359	The Real Tab Book – Vol. 1	$32.50
00240317	The Real Worship Book	$29.99

THE REAL CHRISTMAS BOOK
00240306	C Edition	$25.00
00240345	B♭ Edition	$25.00
00240346	E♭ Edition	$25.00
00240347	Bass Clef Edition	$25.00
00240431	A-G Play-Along CDs	$24.99
00240432	H-M Play-Along CDs	$24.99
00240433	N-Y Play-Along CDs	$24.99

THE REAL VOCAL BOOK
00240230	Volume 1 High Voice	$29.95
00240307	Volume 1 Low Voice	$29.99
00240231	Volume 2 High Voice	$29.95
00240308	Volume 2 Low Voice	$29.95
00240391	Volume 3 High Voice	$29.99
00240392	Volume 3 Low Voice	$29.99

THE REAL BOOK – STAFF PAPER
00240327	$9.95

HOW TO PLAY FROM A REAL BOOK
FOR ALL MUSICIANS
by Robert Rawlins
00312097	$14.99

Complete song lists online at www.halleonard.com
Prices and availability subject to change without notice.

FOR MORE INFORMATION, SEE YOUR LOCAL MUSIC DEALER, OR WRITE TO:

HAL•LEONARD® CORPORATION
7777 W. BLUEMOUND RD. P.O. BOX 13819 MILWAUKEE, WI 53213

1111